- 6 JUN 1994

msc

Journey round the Arctic Circle

Christopher Hill
Su Swallow

The Lutterworth Press
Cambridge

Dedication

In the 1993 United Nations International Year of Indigenous Peoples, I dedicate this book to the Inuit, Saami, and North American and Siberian native peoples, and thank them for their warmth, friendship and understanding in my journey across their Arctic World.

As an asthma sufferer, I should also like to make a dedication to all asthmatic children throughout the world. May they, in the future, find pure air to breathe wherever they live.

Christopher Hill

The Lutterworth Press
P.O. Box 60
Cambridge
CB1 2NT

British Library Cataloguing-in-Publication Data:
A catalogue record is available for this book from the
British Library

First published in Great Britain by The Lutterworth
Press, 1993
Copyright © Christopher Hill and Su Swallow, 1993
ISBN 0 7188 2845 3

Printed in Belgium by Proost

FRONT COVER

Background: *sunset over winter tundra, at the point where Norway, Sweden and Finland meet.*
Central picture: *Alaska traditional fishing, modern transport, among the Yupik people.*
Clockwise from top:
- *keeping warm in the Russian winter.*
- *Inuit girl with whalebone near Eskimo point, Rankin Inlet, Hudson Bay, Canada.*
- *Inuit boy with bone game, Baffin Island.*
- *swimming in a natural hot water lake in Iceland, with a geothermal power station as backdrop.*
- *snowmobile fun in Finland.*

BACK COVER

Background: *the sun bursting through a soft spot in the ozone layer, between Greenland and northern Canada; dangerous ultra-violet rays, which would be absorbed by the ozone layer if it were not damaged by pollution, may cause skin cancer.*
Inset: *Aillohas, the Saami elder who is also an author-artist, an environmentalist and spokeman for the Saami nation, and co-composer of the score for the film Pathfinder as well as a member of the cast.*

FOREWORD BY THE RT HON
LORD SHACKLETON KG, FRS

Christopher Hill's journey around the Arctic Circle was undertaken at a very significant time in the history of the Arctic. It came at a time of great concern at the discovery of environmental damage to the Arctic by man. The Arctic is a unique, pristine, serene wilderness, where the people and ecosystem are under great stress from the pollution of industrialised nations.

In the short space of two years Christopher Hill witnessed in his travels an escalation of the environmental threats to the Arctic. The discovery by international scientists of a hole in the ozone layer, the greenhouse effect, global warming and the possibility of melting ice caps have caused serious alarm. The phenomenon Arctic haze * has changed the colours of sunsets and also creates acid snow and rain. The Saami in Saamiland (Lapland) are still feeling the effects of radiation from the nuclear power station accident at Chernobyl in the former USSR. The Exxon oil spill in Alaska has had serious consequences for the local terrain and wildlife and in Russia industrial waste has caused Arctic rivers and lakes to 'die'.

Let's try and keep the Arctic free from pollution. It is a delicate ecosystem that has taken millions of years to evolve and can give pleasure to generations to come.

I hope that this book will give an insight into what is at stake in the Arctic and that children from all around the world can enjoy and share some of its treasures.

*Arctic haze is caused by smog in the atmosphere being blown by the wind from industrialised countries and accumulating in the Arctic atmosphere.

Lord Shackleton is the son of the celebrated Antarctic explorer Ernest Shackleton. His own expeditions have been to Sarawak and the Arctic as well as the Antarctic. A past President of the Royal Geographical Society, and of the Arctic Club, his publications include Arctic Journeys, *and* Nansen, the Explorer.

ACKNOWLEDGEMENTS

I would like to thank the following people for making this book possible:

ALASKA The people of Kotzebue; Sen. William Hensley. The North Alaska schools and people of Fairbanks; Barbara Short and Bill Stevens.

CANADA The Government of the Northwest Territories, Yellowknife;
The Minister for Education, Hon. Stephen Kakfwi; Director of Operations, Training and Development, Malcolm Farrow.
The Minister for Education, Baffin Island, B. Mentorn.

GREENLAND The school children and teachers at Angmagssalik School.
The Greenland Home Rule, Copenhagen. Morton Larsen.

ICELAND The family Ragnarsson.

SWEDEN/FINLAND/SAAMILAND Karesuando Saami School; Per. G. Kvenangen.
Nils Aslak Valkeapää (Aillohas).
Family Tapio.

RUSSIA The schools and people of Murmansk; Sergei and Ludmilla Belov.
The First Secretary at the Russian Embassy, Mr V Slavin.

LORD SHACKLETON, COLIN MOORE, MIDLAND BANK, THE BRITISH COUNCIL, CAMBRIDGE UNIVERSITY, ROSEMARY DAVIDSON, BBC (SUE LLOYD-ROBERTS), MY FAMILY AND MY FRIEND ANGELA UGLOW FOR BEING THERE AT THE END OF THIS LONG ARCTIC JOURNEY.

PICTURE CREDITS

North West Territories Government, Canada (NWTG): front cover (girl with whalebone), 44 top, centre, 45 top, bottom.
Tessa Macintosh/NWTG: 21 bottom, 28 bottom left, 29 centre, 36 top.
Fran Hurcomb/NWTG: 21 top.
Mike Beedel/NWTG: 35 bottom.
W. Spencer/NWTG: 44 bottom.
Alissa Crandall: 45 centre.
Morten Larsen: front cover (kayak).
Ivanov: 41-43.
All other photographs: Christopher Hill.
Cartoons: Philip Spence.

CONTENTS

The Arctic Circle and Christopher Hill's journey

Key:
        dotted lines show the treeline
        dashed lines show borders between countries
        'North Pole'   = Geographic Pole
        'N.M.P.'   = Magnetic Pole
        DK   = Denmark
        triangles show the points on Christopher Hill's journey:

1-Kotzebue	2-Fairbanks	3-Yellowknife	4-Rankin Inlet
5-Iqaluit	6-Clyde River	7-Angmagssalik	8-Reykjavík
9-Vatnajökull	10-Narvik	11-Karesuando	12-Kemijärvi
13-Murmansk	14-Yakutsk		

INTRODUCTION

Christopher Hill on a snowmobile in front of Kotzebue High School ('Home of the Fighting Huskies') in Alaska.

CHRISTOPHER HILL'S JOURNEY

Christopher Hill travelled on his own over a two-year period around the Arctic Circle, in all seasons. It was a dangerous and difficult journey, sometimes in severe weather conditions in winter, which made photography arduous with weak light and temperatures from -20^{0}C to -68^{0}C. (He even got frostbite once from the steel in his camera, while taking photos of musk ox in Alaska).

The journey encompassed eight countries - Alaska (USA), Canada, Greenland, Iceland, Norway, Sweden, Finland and Russia - and covered a total of over 50,000 miles (80,000 km), travelling on aeroplanes, helicopters and many boats, buses and trains.

Travelling as close to the Arctic Circle as possible, sometimes he would be just below it, on it, or above it in the High Arctic, and he eventually crossed it 17 times.

The journey began one December in a village called Kotzebue, in Alaska on the frozen shores of the Bering Strait, with temperatures around -50^{0}C. Siberia was just a few hundred miles to the west over the pink-tinged hills on the horizon. This was a good place to start a journey - on the International Date Line and the site where a great land-bridge joined Asia to America a few million years ago.

The journey ended in the Russian Arctic in January two years later, during the dark Polar night when the sun does not rise above the horizon. The temperature with the wind chill factor was 68^0 below zero.

Christopher Hill met with Inuit (Eskimos), Indians, Saami (Lapps), Icelanders and many Russian Arctic ethnic groups from all walks of life: doctors, teachers, students, children, miners, fishermen, engineers, airmen, border guards, military, environmentalists, artists and musicians, sailors on the nuclear ice-breakers, housewives, hunters and trappers. He had encounters with whales, musk ox, caribou, golden eagles, reindeer and lynx. He drifted in small dinghys amongst icebergs off Greenland, bumped over the snow on skidoos and travelled with sledge and huskies.

The hospitality and warmth of the people he met in the north and their profound respect for the wilderness of the Arctic regions greatly impressed him. In sharing this Arctic experience, Christopher Hill hopes to encourage a deeper understanding of the earth and the world in which we live.

ALASKA

KOTZEBUE

These Inuit children go to the Kotzebue School for Fighting Huskies. The school does not open when the temperature drops below -30°C.

Our journey round the Arctic Circle begins in a large Eskimo village called Kotzebue. It is on the west coast of Alaska, beside the Chuckchi Sea. It is winter and the sea is frozen.

When you walk down the street by the shore, it is difficult to see where the land ends and the sea begins because both are covered in ice and snow. The cold wind brings the temperature down from -30°C to -75°C.

When the ice breaks up, in spring, the Inuit will be able to use their boats for fishing. But from October to April the villagers race across the sea ice on skidoos to go ice-fishing. They cut a hole in the thick ice and dangle a spinner in the water below to attract the fish, which they catch and tow home on a sledge. Some families keep husky dogs to pull their sledge although they have snow vehicles as well. The dogs are often more reliable on long hunting trips.

For most of the Inuit who live in Kotzebue, their way of life is a mixture of old and new. They still hunt and fish for much of their food - seals, salmon, walrus, whales, caribou and even polar bears - but nowadays they use rifles instead of bows and arrows and harpoons. In

This is Shore Avenue, beside the sea. The antlers piled up on the roof of one of the houses come from caribou.

8

summer, fish and strips of meat are dried ready for the winter, but tea, coffee and tinned fruit can be bought in the local store, and there is even a 24-hour pizza restaurant.

Many of the Inuit children learn the traditional crafts of carving and embroidery from their parents, but they also spend many hours on dark winter days listening to the radio or playing basketball. Basketball is so popular that children sometimes miss school to watch a local tournament. In school, the children are taught in English, but at home they will usually speak Inupiat, one of the Eskimo languages.

If you move away from the seashore and into the village, the street names give you a clue about which animals live in this region of the Arctic: Grizzly Street, Fox Way, Wolverine Drive, Caribou Drive. Herds of caribou often pass near to Kotzebue on their summer journey to the north, returning south in winter. When they do, men from the village set off across many miles of deserted tundra to find them. The meat will feed their families for weeks to come, and the skins are used to make the traditional parkas, which are much warmer than modern nylon coats.

If you visit other Eskimo groups in Alaska, such as the Yupiks in the south, you will hear a different language and see different landscapes,

A little girl watches her mother as she fishes for tomcod and sheefish through a hole in the ice.

but the way of life is very similar. The Indians who live in Alaska also have a lot in common with the Eskimo. The next stop on our Arctic journey is Fairbanks, the second largest city in the state and home to some of the Athabascan native people who live in the interior, as the middle of Alaska is called. There are no roads or railways out of Kotzebue, so we go by air.

Caribou have to search under the snow for mosses and lichens to eat.

Cross-country sledging is fun! A team of four or six husky dogs pull the sledge, which is made out of birch wood.

FAIRBANKS

Fairbanks lies in a valley between two great mountain ranges. From the plane you can see a swirling pattern of rivers, frozen white because it is winter, and all leading into one very wide river, the Yukon. In the past, small groups of Athabascan native Americans lived beside these rivers, finding food by hunting, fishing and gathering berries. Some still live like this in tiny villages of log cabins, miles from anywhere. Others live in the city, which grew up at the beginning of the century when the white people came looking for gold.

Today most of the gold mines are closed, and Fairbanks now thrives on 'black gold' - oil. When oil was discovered on the north coast of Alaska, Fairbanks was an ideal stop-off point on the journey to and from the oil fields. People came from all over the world to work there, or to build the trans-Alaska pipeline, which carries the oil south to the port at Valdez ready for shipping.

The pipeline, which passes close to Fairbanks, runs on stilts above the ground. It could not have been buried in the ground because even in summer the earth below the surface stays frozen - this layer of frozen earth is called permafrost - which makes building difficult. In Fairbanks itself you can see lopsided houses

ALASKA OIL PIPELINE
The Trans-Alaska pipeline runs from north to south 800 miles (1,300 km) from Prudhoe Bay across the Arctic Circle, past Mount McKinley the highest mountain in North America (20,320 ft or 6,190 m high), over the tundra, permafrost and forest until it reaches Valdez at the Gulf of Alaska. The average pipeline output is two million barrels a day.

The oil pipeline from Prudhoe Bay in the north to Valdez in the south, is the longest in North America.

10

An Athabascan Indian fiddler plays in the school hall. The mural on the wall is a reminder of the designs once painted on house walls.

whose foundations have been damaged by the permafrost. Ice fog is another problem for city-dwellers in the Arctic; when it is very cold, the air just above the ground turns into a fog of tiny ice crystals, which in turn trap car fumes and factory smoke.

One way to escape the fog and warm up is to bathe in the hot springs outside Fairbanks, just as the first gold miners did nearly 100 years ago. You can drive there, provided you take a survival kit in case the car breaks down, but there are few roads out of Fairbanks. In summer, of course, you can explore the area by boat. Then you might see Indians paddling their canoes and fishing for salmon. In winter, when the rivers are frozen, the only way to travel long distances is by plane. Small, one-engine planes, fitted with skis for landing on ice, carry mail, food, medicines and five or six

passengers to the 'bush'. The bush is anywhere in Alaska that has no roads. Fairbanks has become headquarters for bush pilots, who brave blizzards and ice fog to reach tiny, remote villages, and sometimes to rescue mountain climbers or stranded explorers.

One evening we are invited to a *potlatch*, a kind of family party where Indians from several villages meet up. We travel by sledge, pulled along by a team of eight dogs. The driver carries a leather whip, and cries 'Musch! Musch!' to make the dogs go faster. Sledges are used for travel and for fun - sledge racing is a very popular sport in Alaska. One of the longest races in the world, the Iditarod, takes place here - it covers 1,000 miles (1,609 km) and lasts for two weeks!

Musk Ox: shaggy, stocky, long-haired mammals found in Greenland, Siberia, Alaska and Canada. Their warm underfur, 'qivuit', is used as knitting yarn. When attacked by wolves they form a circle with the young in the middle.

11

At the *potlatch*, everyone gathers outside round a huge wood fire, trading goods they have brought and describing their latest hunting trips. When the music starts - there is a violin, a guitar and a drum - people start to sing and dance.

If you want to find out what life is like for the Indians who still live in the bush, you can fly out to a log cabin for a few days. You will have to cut wood every day to keep the stove alight, trudging over the snow on snowshoes. A local fur trapper might whizz past you on a dog sledge or a snow machine, hoping to find a red fox, a snowshoe hare or a muskrat caught in his traps.

Daylight lasts for only four hours in the cabin, and then you have to work by the light of an oil lantern. The Indians use this time to mend

sledges and canoes, and to make clothing from animal fur. You might make a pair of *mukluks* to keep your feet warm - boots made from moose hide, trimmed with fur and decorated with tiny glass beads.

Life is not quite so hard for the Athabascan Indians who live in Fairbanks itself. They may work in a factory or a mine during the week, and have electricity and running water in their homes. At the weekends, however, many leave the city to go hunting in the bush and others make baskets and clothes in the traditional style. You might like to buy a basket made from birch bark, or a pair of beaded fur mittens as a souvenir of your visit, before you set off across the frontier into Canada.

Alaskan Indians carve totem poles in memory of their ancestors and to worship their gods.

CANADA

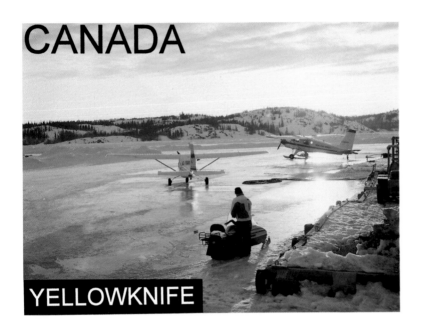

YELLOWKNIFE

The vast green forests of northern Canada are broken up by a patchwork of lakes and rivers, where you can sail in the summer and skate in the winter. Our next stop is in Yellowknife, the capital of the North-West Territories. The town sits beside the Great Slave Lake, which is fed by the huge Mackenzie River.

The Indians or Dene have fished in the waters and hunted in the forests of the North-West Territories for hundreds of years. Many Dene tribes, such as Dogrib, Cree and others still spend at least part of the year fishing for trout, pike and char, and hunting moose, deer and bear. Each catch is shared out between the families in the camp, where the women stretch and scrape clean the animal skins ready to be made into moccasins or mitts, decorated with porcupine quills. In the past, the skins were also used to cover the stick frame of the Indian teepee. Teepees nowadays are made of canvas.

U/V WARNINGS
In Canada the daily weather forecasts on the radio and television now include details of levels of ultra-violet radiation, monitored by weather stations. The broadcasts warn parents and children when levels are dangerously high, so they can take protective measures to avoid the danger of getting skin cancer.

Dene boys welcome a visitor to their school with songs and drum music, played on drums of caribou skin.

Dene children enjoy playing on the frozen Great Slave Lake. The sun is bright, but it is very cold: -30°C.

Few Dene live permanently in teepees. Most live in small, wooden houses, with running water and electricity, in villages like Detah, on the Great Slave Lake. In winter, you can reach the village from Yellowknife by following the ice road across the lake. In summer, there is a ferry across the Mackenzie River. But twice a year, in the great spring thaw and the autumn freeze, the crossing is too dangerous by any means and Yellowknife is cut off from southern Canada. There have been accidents: a digger once crashed through the ice and a helicopter had to haul it back to land.

In winter, though, the lake is a wonderful ice playground, where the children race snowmobiles round markers, and roll old lorry tyres across the ice - if they went from one end to the other they would have to keep going for 300 miles (480 km)! They go fishing and catch pike, char and trout through holes in the ice.

All the children in Detah attend the village school, where they learn French, English and their own language. Most road signs and newspapers are in both French and English. Radio and television programmes are in either French or English and in one of the aboriginal languages.

At home, Indian families mostly use their own language. Parents and grandparents tell the children about the time when they were young. They remember a very different life, when everyone moved from camp to camp in the bush, often very cold and hungry, sometimes in danger, but always enjoying a life of freedom, of sharing food and shelter and caring for the land. They are sad that some of the old ways of life are disappearing. But they are glad about some of the new ways too. They are pleased about the schools, for example, and nursing stations for health care.

If you spend a day at the school, you will find some of the old traditions are kept alive. The smell of freshly baked bannock bread tells the children it is nearly lunchtime. Bannock was brought to Canada from Scotland by the whalers and traders who arrived here 200 years ago. After lunch, some of the older pupils practise playing the drums, which are made from caribou skin stretched over a wooden frame. The boys play hunting songs and dance music. For the Dene and Inuit, the drum has magical powers. The shaman - who is a sort of priest - uses the drum to communicate with religious spirits.

Magic certainly seems to be in the air on those nights when the Aurora Borealis (northern lights) fills the dark sky with green, yellow, red or purple light. It is not surpris-ing that people invented all kinds of stories to explain these curtains of colour, before scientists discovered that they appear when the sun's rays come into contact with the earth's magnetic field. But don't worry if you do not catch sight of the northern lights while you are here. You will certainly get a chance to see them somewhere else on your way round the Arctic Circle. Apart from Dene, the North-West Territories are also inhabited by Inuit (one of the peoples who are sometimes called Eskimos). The Cana-dian Government in 1993 created a large new Territory for the Inuit in this area. It is called Nunavut - 'our land' in the Inuktitut tongue. The area, all of which is above the treeline, is shown on the map on p.6.

Pupils at the Detah village school often help to make bannock bread for their lunch.

COMMERCIAL WHALING
Many of the species of whale are faced with extinction as a result of commercial whaling. But whaling on a small scale by some indigenous peoples on the coast is central to their way of life and poses no threat.

BAFFIN ISLAND

We have flown 1,800 miles to the east, to Baffin Island. It is north of the Arctic Circle and north of the tree line, so the only trees that grow here are a few tiny dwarf willows, a few inches high. This kind of landscape is called the tundra; only mosses, lichens and very low-growing plants survive here. For now, even they are hidden under the snow and ice. In the bay where the frozen Clyde River meets the sea, glaciers sparkle in the sun and canoes with outboard motors sit beside blue icebergs, trapped in the ice until late spring.

The villages dotted along the coast of Baffin Bay are home to Inuit, who in many ways live just like the first Inuit who settled here 2,000 years ago. If you find a ring of stones, it is not a magic circle but the ancient site of a summer house, a tent of caribou or seal skin that was weighted down with those stones against winds of up to 80 miles per hour (130 km p.h.) Some Inuit still like to live in skin or canvas tents as well as in the wooden houses provided by the government, dividing their time between the two.

This traditional tent stands on the sea ice. The skins are stiched together and pulled over a frame of wooden struts which are pushed into the ice.

These children sometimes help their father to hunt seals. A sealskin is being stretched and dried outside their house, ready to be made into clothes.

Piles of whale bones are another clue to the past. In winter, Inuit used to live in sod huts, made from slabs of turf laid on a frame of whale bones; or the bones might have been left behind by European whalers who hunted off this coast 100 years ago. Today, these weathered bones are good for carving ornaments, which will be sold to tourists who come to ski on the glaciers, to fish and to go hiking in the mountains.

An Inuit community used to be able to live on one whale for a year. They used its bones for housebuilding, its meat for food, and its blubber for oil which could be burned to provide heat and light. The skin, called *muktuk*, is a delicacy even today. It is full of vitamin C and tastes a bit like coconut. The Inuit still hunt beluga whales, which are not endangered, but the number they are allowed to catch is controlled to protect these mammals. Seals provide meat both for people and dogs, and their skins are sold to make *kamiks* - boots - and mitts, to keep out the cold.

The seal meat is essential to these people who live in a land where it is too cold to grow vegetables or cereal crops. They kill no more than they have to in order to survive, and take only adult seals. Thus, they show respect for the animals they depend on for their livelihood.

Children learn Inuktitut writing at school. They also learn English and French.

INUIT CIRCUMPOLAR CONFERENCE (I.C.C.) for Canadian, American and Greenland Inuit. An economic and cultural organisation based on the sensible use of renewable resources (hunting, fishing, hydroelectric power, mining and gas). It was formed to help maintain the Inuit spirit.

A mother collects her child from the Clyde River school.

While the men of Clyde River village are out hunting, the children are at school, using computers, watching a television programme from Iqaluit, or practising the Inuit writing. But no one wants to stay in school when the fog has cleared and the sun is shining. It is time to go on an Arctic picnic. A sledge is loaded up with food, a kettle and an oil burner, and the children set off across the frozen bay on skidoos. The snow spray blown up by the skidoo in front freezes on their cheeks.

Everyone is glad when they reach the chosen spot, about 12 miles away. While some of the boys play baseball, others race each other down the mountain slopes, toboggans and snowmobiles, closely matched at speeds of 15 or 20 miles per hour/25 or 30 km p.h. For a while, you don't notice the temperature, -40^{0}C, but when you stop to eat, your numb hands fumble to pick up strips of dried fish (Arctic char) and caribou, cubes of raw seal meat and fresh bannock bread.

High Arctic Tundra.

TUNDRA
An area of flat plains between the ice cap and the tree-line in Arctic regions, where there are almost no trees and where the ground is permanently frozen just below the surface. Only small plants with short roots can grow, such as lichens, mosses and stunted shrubs.

Tundra is known as the 'barren lands' in Canada).

Polar bears can be dangerous when they are hungry, so on the picnic one boy armed with a rifle keeps a look out.

Innugaq is a children's game which is played at school and at home. The players make pictures with seal flipper bones and tell a story to go with the picture.

The Inuit diet of fish and meat is high in fat and helps to keep out the bitter cold. This same diet, together with their thick fur, helps animals like the polar bear to survive in the Arctic too. Thousands of bears hunt along the coast, eating a seal a day if they can, but able to survive for up to six months without food if necessary. If food is scarce, they sometimes raid villages, searching rubbish dumps and even houses looking for scraps. A hungry bear can be dangerous, so even on the picnic one of the boys has a rifle, just in case. A week ago, a hungry polar bear came into the school playground and had to be shot. Normally, unless a bear threatens to attack, it will be left in peace. The people of Clyde River village are allowed to kill only eight bears each year for meat and fur.

Animal fur is used for clothing, and for bedding. Inside a traditional house or qarmak a raised wooden platform covered with furs is the family bed where everyone sleeps close together for warmth. When we visit a qarmak, the children are sitting on the bed playing a game called *innugaq*, which means seal flipper bones. To play the game you have to hook the bones out of a sealskin mitten, and tell a story about the shapes you can make with them: a hut, a dog team, a hunter and so on. When the game is finished, it is time to continue our journey.

Some Inuit families spend at least part of the year in tents. The seal-oil lamp (or stove) is used for cooking, heating and light.

Food and eating in the Arctic

Meat and fish form the staple diet of most people who live round the Arctic Circle. Berries are collected during the short summer. Crops can only be grown in a few places because the ground below the surface is permanently frozen. Arctic peoples generally prefer their traditional diet - it helps them to survive in the very harsh climate - although all kinds of other foods are now often available at the local supermarket.

In Yellowknife, North-West Territories, Canada, baked Arctic char and stewed cranberries make up a typical evening meal.

Inuit and Indian women use a knife called an ulu to cut meat such as bison and caribou, which is eaten both raw and cooked.

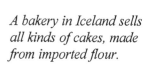

A bakery in Iceland sells all kinds of cakes, made from imported flour.

Fish caught in the summer are dried in the sun and stored in a wooden cache ready for the winter. This scene is on the banks of the Mackenzie River, in northern Canada.

The diet of northern native peoples is mainly meat and fish. Few vegetables grow in an Arctic climate.

These children in Greenland are given a taste of the seal stew their mother is preparing.

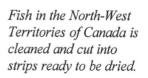

Fish in the North-West Territories of Canada is cleaned and cut into strips ready to be dried.

GREENLAND

The East Greenland coast in autumn.

By the time we fly to Greenland, the short Arctic summer has begun. From the air we can see the bare rocky coastline running round the edge of the island, the largest island in the world. But even in summer, 80% of the country is covered in ice and the sea is dotted with icebergs which have broken away from the glaciers.

Before the first explorers came to Greenland, some of the Inuit who lived here were so isolated that they thought they were the only people alive on earth. The Inuit of eastern Greenland were first discovered by a Danish explorer and were once governed by Denmark. The Danes have made many changes to the traditional Inuit way of life. They set up schools, built large blocks of flats, set up fish factories and built hospitals. They brought sheep to the island, and about 80 families now look after about 40,000 animals, which are raised for their meat.

Some of the changes obviously helped the Inuit people, but the traditional way of life was in danger of disappearing. Now Greenland has its own parliament in Nuuk, the capital, and many Inuit have combined the old way of life with some of today's modern conveniences such as electricity and running water. There is no local television station but they can hire video cassettes.

Icebergs drift in and out of Kulusuk fjord, to be frozen in place as autumn sets in. Greenland has very little soil and, in the churchyard, bodies have to be buried under rocks. The bodies remain frozen for ever in the permafrost.

*Morten and Maliaraq live in a modern
Danish-style house but they both enjoy
Inuit cooking and crafts.*

There are no railways in Greenland, and not many roads, so we arrive by plane. A helicopter takes us on the next stage of our journey to the village of Angmagssalik, on the east coast of Greenland, where we will stay with a family. Morten is Danish, and teaches maths at the local school. His wife, Maliaraq, is Inuit. Their modern, Scandinavian-style house is full of reminders of the Inuit way of life. A polar bear skull, a seal skin, brightly coloured beadwork and a calendar of hunting scenes decorate the living room. On our first evening, Maliaraq finishes a traditional costume for one of her daughters to wear on her birthday, and Morten cleans his rifle ready for a hunting trip.

The sea ice has broken up, so the skidoos and dog sledges have been set aside and boats sit in the little harbour ready for the fishermen. Some people still use kayaks: one-man canoes made from a wood or bone frame covered with seal-skin or canvas. Like most people in the village, Morten has a motorboat. One afternoon, we set off across the bay with our fishing gear and a rifle. What will we return with? Perhaps a sea bird or two, a shark, a seal or even a walrus. This is, after all, the time of year when these heavy relatives of the seals climb on to the ice to raise their young calves. The meat would feed the family and the dogs, and its ivory tusks could be carved into ornaments for sale.

In the end, though, it is not a walrus we see but something much more impressive. As the sun begins to set, the dark, glistening back of a fin whale rises out of the water only a few

*Wildflowers burst
into life during the
brief summer, filling
the valley with colour
until the ground
freezes over again.*

23

Greenland has no roads or railways, and few runways for planes. Most short, inland trips are by sledge or helicopter. Sledges are used for hunting and transporting goods.

metres away from our tiny boat, which rocks and tips dangerously. With a loud hiss as it blows out air, the huge beautiful creature sinks slowly below the surface. If it comes any closer, we will be tipped into the sea. In water just above freezing point, even the best swimmer cannot survive for more than ten or fifteen minutes. We wait, not speaking or moving. Suddenly, the whale reappears a little further away, and seems to salute us as it slaps the water with its tail. The ripples it makes, three perfect circles, move out towards us.

We start the engine and cut through the rings of water, heading for home. It is nearly dark, but light enough to see another shape cutting through the water - the fin of a killer whale. One way these creatures catch their prey is by pushing up an ice floe to tip off a seal which may be resting on the ice. The whale could do the same with our boat. It is a great relief to get back to the shore safely, even though there is no catch for supper.

As we drag the boat up to the stony beach, it is impossible to ignore the rubbish that litters the shore - empty oil drums, household waste, rusting machine parts. Getting rid of rubbish is a real problem in a land where the permafrost makes it difficult to dig more than a few inches into the ground. Much of the rubbish is taken inland and dumped in natural craters.

It is very cold as we walk back to the village. Even in summer the temperature is rarely above 10°C, but at least the storm winds are still. In winter, a fierce wind called the *piteraq* blows down from the North Pole and sends the temperature down to -75°C. The local weather station, which is also a radar beacon for planes that cross the Atlantic, sounds the siren when the *piteraq* blows. Then it is time to stay indoors, away from the flying debris. Ten years ago the local school was completely blown away in just one afternoon!

Before winter returns, it is time to continue our journey, to another island whose very name makes you feel cold.

View of the village of Angmagssalik

NORTH POLE

The northern end of the Earth's axis of rotation is called the Geographic North Pole. Magnetic north is the direction of the Earth's magnetic pole, and a compass needle always points in its direction. See p.6.

ICELAND

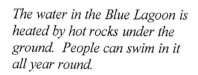
A heavy mist hangs over land that is part of a sheep farm.

If you were a polar bear you might float across to Iceland from Greenland on drift ice carried by the warm waters of the Gulf Stream. Sometimes so much ice drifts down the Gulf Stream that the harbours become blocked and ships cannot enter until the ice floats away again. Like most visitors, though, we have not come by ice or by ship, but by plane.

From the air, Iceland looks a bit like the moon - rocky and bare with craters. As we come in to land, we can see bright green fields spread out beside icy blue glaciers, and then black lava fields beyond. A volcano could erupt here at any time, and even burst through the thick ice of the glacier, spraying it with more lava. Out to sea, the new island of Surtsey is still growing as lava is thrown up from an underwater volcano, the hot rock sizzling and steaming as it falls back into icy water. On the mainland, however, the world's most active volcanic region is quiet.

At the airport we are met by Erik Ragnarsson (meaning son of Ragar) and Selma Gudmundsdottir (meaning daughter of Gudmund). They take us to the Blue Lagoon. It is like a huge outdoor swimming pool. The hot water comes from under the ground, where the volcanic rock heats the rainwater to boiling point as it drains through the soil. Orange markers in the lagoon show clearly where it is too hot to swim. Swimming is one of Iceland's most popular sports, and children have to take swimming tests at school.

The water in the Blue Lagoon is heated by hot rocks under the ground. People can swim in it all year round.

Hot water lies just below the surface in Iceland. Holes are the remains of old geysers, where the water once bubbled and steamed out of the ground.

'NATURAL' ENERGY
Iceland produces most of its energy and hot water from natural resources. Hot water for central heating comes from geo-thermal energy such as volcanic activity. Electricity is generated by harnessing the energy of rivers and waterfalls.

Most people in Iceland live very close to hot water, which bubbles away only three or four metres below the ground. In some places hot springs shoot up into the air and steam rises from holes in the ground like hundreds of kettles on the boil - but the steam can scald, so beware!

The hot water from the ground is pumped through pipes to most houses for central heating and hot water. The water is also used to heat greenhouses, where you could pick cucumbers, tomatoes and bunches of flowers. You can also find grapes, figs and even bananas, except in winter when there are not enough hours of daylight to grow exotic fruits. Heat from the underground water is also used to make electricity, and fish farms use the hot water to breed and grow fish. Geothermal energy - using heat from the ground - is very important in Iceland. The supply of hot water is never-ending and it is a clean source of energy that does not pollute the atmosphere.

Steam rising from the ground must have surprised the first settlers in Iceland. When the Vikings arrived from Norway they called one place Reykjavik, which means 'smoke bay'. It is now the capital of Iceland. Like most towns in Iceland, it is modern, with all kinds of shops, and a surprising number of book shops.

Tomatoes, palms, and even bananas are grown in this greenhouse in a semitropical atmosphere provided by hot steam from underground.

Children growing vegetables in Iceland, one of the few places on the Arctic Circle where this can be done.

These girls are collecting potatoes which they have grown themselves.

Icelanders read a lot of books. Some of the most precious books are not for sale. They are kept in a museum in Reykjavík. They are the sagas (stories about Iceland) written in the old Norse language of the Vikings. They are written on vellum, a kind of parchment made from animal skin.

If you arrive in Iceland at the same time as us, you will find the schoolchildren enjoying their long summer holiday, which lasts four months. The older children often spend the time working, perhaps in a wool factory or on a farm. Many children have their own plot where they grow vegetables, which must be harvested before winter sets in. In their free time they play chess or football, ride on the Icelandic ponies or go salmon fishing.

Before we leave this land of ice and fire, we must visit the docks where men are busy unloading crates of cod from the trawlers. Sea fishing is the main industry in Iceland. You will find fish on every restaurant menu in Iceland. You could try shark with melon, or lamb with halibut, but an everyday meal would be baked cod or raw herring and vegetables, with a cake for pudding. Iceland exports most of its fish, usually frozen or salted to countries such as America and Africa.

From Reykjavík we go across Iceland by road to Seydisfjördur, where we will board a ship bound for Bergen, in Norway. On the way to the port we pass some of the most startling scenery on our Arctic journey. First there is Vatnajökull, the biggest glacier in Europe. Then there are the black deserts of lava ash and lakes dotted with black icebergs, and in between there are gushing waterfalls which make double and even triple rainbows in the sunlight.

The day's catch is sold as soon as the fisherman return to harbour. Cod is the most important fish for Iceland.

27

Crafts and Clothes

Beadwork, basket-making and carving are a few of the crafts which older people still teach their children, in the hope that the skills will not be lost as modern, machine made goods become available.

Mukluks - sealskin boots made by the Inuit - are warm and waterproof.

An Inuit lady in Greenland, wearing clothes decorated with beads, is making a pair of sealskin boots.

The traditional costume in Iceland is decorated with fine silverwork.

Indian clothes are often patterned with coloured porcupine quills and beads.

Lace-making, metalwork and wood-carving are among the crafts found in Russia.

Canadian Indians use the bark of birch trees to make baskets.

These carvings from Greenland are made of bone, stone and wood. As there are no trees on the island, people collect driftwood or use imported timber. Ivory from the tusks of walrus and narwhal is also for carving.

NORWAY

A fishing village sits along the coastline in a fjord near Narvik.

We are going to travel north through Norway to a town called Narvik. We could go up the coast by steamship. Even in winter the Norwegian Sea does not completely freeze and ships can move freely. This time, however, we go by bus, following the main road that winds past fields and lakes and mountains.

In the north, the country is long and very narrow, only a few miles across in places, with the sea on one side and the Swedish border on the other. The coast is a jagged line with fjords (inlets) that cut deep into the land. To cross the fjords there are bridges and car ferries. Some children have to use the car ferry to get to and from their school on the other side of the fjord.

Narvik is at the head of a large fjord where 50 years ago many ships were sunk in battles in the Second World War. Today ships sail from Norway carrying iron ore that has been mined on the Swedish side of the border. The iron ore is brought through the mountains from Sweden by train - Narvik is the most northern railway station in Europe. We are going to cross into Sweden by train. This will be our first train journey since we began to explore the Arctic Circle.

As the train passes through the mountains, we can clearly see ski tracks left on the snow, but there is no one in sight. We have left the fir trees behind and are now moving towards the edge of the flat tundra, where lichens and mosses and dwarf silver birch grow close to the ground. It all looks very still and quiet. Then a golden eagle swoops into view, plunging down on a white Arctic hare. The eagle tears at its prey, the blood staining the snow, and two black ravens arrive to finish the eagle's meal.

This remote area is very near to the lands inhabited by the Saami people. The Saami live in the very north of Norway, Sweden and Finland and in the Kola Peninsula in Russia. It is a vast wilderness which used to be called Lapland but is now called Saamiland.

Some of the best fishing grounds are off the northern coast of Norway.

The Saami have herded reindeer for 400 years. Today, only a few keep reindeer, but most of them try to keep their language and old way of life alive.

If you could spend a year with a Saami family who kept reindeer, you would find that they live a different kind of year to yours. Their life is controlled by the changes in the weather and the needs of the reindeer. So while we have only four seasons, every change in the weather is a new season to them and every time the herd moves to find new food, the Saami go too. In early spring, children help their parents to lasso the family's 200 or 300 animals, which have spent the winter with other reindeer in a huge fenced enclosure. The females are easier to catch than the males because they still have their antlers. The males have their antlers sawn off to stop them hurting each other when they fight. The herd is taken to grazing land in the mountains or by the coast, away from the mosquitoes which are such a pest in the Arctic summer.

HOLE IN THE OZONE LAYER
The gases (chlorofluorocarbons) which make aerosol sprays work and which are used to cool fridges are collecting in the atmosphere and thinning the ozone layer that protects living things from the most dangerous rays of the sun.

As long as there is snow on the ground, the Saami follow their reindeer on snowmobiles, or on skis - which the Saami invented. They eat reindeer meat and catch fish in the lakes, and set up their skin coloured tents for sleeping. When the snow begins to thaw during the day, the herders travel at night when the snow freezes over again and is easier to walk on. The journey lasts many days. The Saami have no maps to guide them through the wilderness. Each year they find their way by following small natural landmarks - a rock, a dwarf tree, a small hillock.

We will hear more of the reindeer herds and their herders later.

By now we are approaching Kiruna, in Sweden. Steam and smoke rise up from the iron ore mines hidden behind the hills, where many local people work. Above the noise of the freight trains carrying the iron ore we can hear dogs barking from the gardens alongside the railway. Dog sledge racing is a favourite sport in this town, but we will not have time to see a race. We have a bus to catch.

SWEDEN

*Aillohas, who usually wears Saami costume, works here
in his studio, which has a sauna next door.*

The bus from Kiruna goes very slowly over the icy roads, past the weather station where a huge satellite dish tracks the hole in the ozone layer in the Arctic sky. The temperature outside is -20°C. Tonight, when the bus is parked, it will be plugged into an electricity supply to keep the engine warm and stop it from freezing up.

The bus stops in every tiny village, taking shoppers and schoolchildren home from the town. It takes us eight hours to reach the village of Karesuando, where we will stay with a Saami family.

We meet a group of Saami: Aillohas, Liselott, Inger and Per. They all live in warm modern houses and drive Volvo cars but they have a Saami teepee outside, and their cache for frozen meat is hidden among the birch trees.

Aillohas wears bright Saami clothes, and reindeer slippers stuffed with soft dry grass.

As we eat, the Saami radio news warns that children in the southern part of Saamiland should not pick berries there. They are still contaminated with radioactive material which blew across from the Chernobyl nuclear power station at the time of the accident there in 1986.

Aillohas tells us more about the herding cycle of reindeer.

FALLOUT FROM NUCLEAR POWER STATIONS

In Saamiland, the Chernobyl accident in 1986 has caused a big problem for those in northern Finland and Scandanavia. Radioactive dust fell in rain and snow into lakes and rivers, and onto the grazing land so plants, fishes and even reindeer who ate the grass were contaminated.

Some Saami still herd reindeer for a living. The meat and skins provide food and clothing and the antlers are used for carvings and knife handles.

When the calves are born, on the way to the summer camp, a small piece is cut out of one ear to show whom they belong to. Each family has its own pattern, and the cut-out pieces are kept as a record of how many calves have been born. Everyone keeps a special watch at calving time in case the reindeer are chased by hungry lynx or wolverine.

There is time to relax a little at the summer camp. This is the land of the 'midnight sun', when the sun does not set for several weeks during the summer. The light evenings are spent round the fire singing *joiks* (a jazzy kind of song that expresses the events of the day) to the sound of a drum, a reindeer skin stretched over a carved wooden frame and beaten with a piece of antler.

Then, as spring approaches, the whole herding cycle begins again. It is not an easy life for the Saami reindeer herders, and it is made more difficult as new roads, dams and mines cut into the land roamed by the reindeer.

After a short stay with the Saami, we are off across the river border into Finland. The bus has to stop at intervals to allow reindeer to cross the road, their milk-chocolate-coloured fur standing out against the snow. One or two have white fur. These will fetch the best prices when the hides are sold to make clothes. Later, the bus stops in the middle of nowhere to allow a . Saami to get on. He is in traditional costume and carrying the traditional Saami knife with a handle carved from bone. A little further on and we reach the border.

The design by Lisa Tapio on the bag of reindeer skin tells the story of the Chernobyl disaster. A girl stands with her arms outstretched as a dark cloud of radiation covers the sun.

FINLAND

Many children ski to school. This school in Kemiev is only five miles from the Russian border.

Some people say that Father Christmas lives in Finland, north of the Arctic Circle. You may not see him in Rovaneimi, but you will see a giant picture of him outside a supermarket there. Inside the store you can buy everything from birch bark baskets to frozen reindeer meat.

This town is only 350 miles (560 km) from the Saami village in Sweden, but it feels like a different world. The modern shops and busy streets full of traffic could be in England, except for the bitter cold - which no amount of fur seems to keep out.

Finland is called the land of a thousand lakes. We pass a few on our way east round the Arctic Circle to Kemijavi, a town near the Russian border. When the lakes are frozen, as they are now, they become huge playgrounds for children who race their skidoos across the ice, play ice hockey and go cross-country skiing. One girl has made a flying saucer out of ice and snow and says she might fly across the border to Russia! We want to cross the border too, but need a visa. Only wild animals can travel freely over a country's borders.

Racing skidoos across the ice.

Reindeer antler which is used for decoration or carving, or for drumsticks.

In the local school the children learn about the animals that live in this part of the world. One of the corridors is lined with glass cases full of wild animals that have been preserved. The birds of prey - white-tailed eagles, buzzards, falcons - look very fierce.

Outside the school, it is hard to forget the cold. A popular way to warm up in Finland is to have a sauna, a hot steam bath. Most houses have a pine-wood sauna room, where you sprinkle water on to hot rocks to make lots of steam. If you get too hot you can go outside and roll in the snow to cool off!

Most houses on the border also have satellite television and can receive Swedish, Finnish, Norwegian and Russian programmes. Before we leave Finland we watch a weather forecast from Russia. It is difficult to read in a different alphabet, but we do recognise:

САНКТ-ПЕТЕРБУРГ

(St Petersburg)

which is the next place on our journey round the Arctic Circle.

AURORA BOREALIS
Ribbons of coloured lights that can occur in the Arctic sky caused by particles from the sun coming into contact with the Earth's magnetic field.

No visit to the Arctic Circle would be complete without a glimpse of the Aurora Borealis or northern lights, which fill the sky with streaks and swirls of green, yellow and red.

TRAVEL AND TRANSPORT

In summer, planes fitted with floats can land on lakes to pick up passengers - a doctor or teacher going into the tundra perhaps, or a family off to visit relatives. This one is in Yellowknife, Canada.

Outside cities, Soviet people often use skis to travel from village to village.

These children in Fairbanks are enjoying a husky-and-sledge trip.

A snow motorbike is often the best way to travel in the winter. This lady has taken the short cut across the sea ice to the local store in the Bering Straits near Alaska. In the background you can see Siberia, across the international dateline.

The train that runs between Fairbanks and Anchorage - the only train in Alaska - passes through Denali Wildlife Park, where bears and elks are sometimes killed as they cross the railway line.

When the boats are frozen in for the winter, huskies and other dogs are used to pull sledges across the ice. This, too, is the Bering Straits, where the continents of Asia and North America are joined by ice. You could walk across!

RUSSIA

MURMANSK

Tobogganing in the park at Murmansk during the polar night.

When we crossed the border from Finland into the Russian Federation (at that time, part of the Soviet Union), we had no idea that we would soon be sharing a meal with a young Russian border guard. Igor travelled with us aboard the Arctic Express, on the 30 hour journey north from St Petersburg to Murmansk.

The express, a very long wide-gauge train, is quite luxurious, with oriental carpets in the corridor and tea served in silver cups. Each carriage is heated by a boiler, looked after by a tea lady. She fills the boiler with coal, and keeps the water on the boil for endless cups of *chai* (tea).

There is no restaurant on the train, so we have all brought our own food. We have sandwiches and some English chocolate. Igor offers us sausage and bread, and sugared hazelnuts. A little vodka, made from wheat or potatoes, helps to keep out the cold. This is the first time Igor has met English people. He is surprised that we have so much news about Russia in our newspapers and on television. We talk about the changes going on here.

On the island of Novaya Zemlya, in the Russian Arctic, nuclear testing and dumping of radio-active materials on land and sea could have catastrophic consequences for wildlife and people along the Norwegian and Russian coast.

All day long, English and Russian pop music plays through loudspeakers up and down the train. If you want more entertainment, you can visit the cinema compartment, where a Mickey

The Arctic Express makes the 30 hour journey from Murmansk to St Petersburg twice a week.

Children on their way home from school stop to play on the castle of ice in the town square.

Mouse video might be shown on the huge television screen. Many people, though, pass the time reading, or playing cards or chess. Some passengers walk about in their pyjamas, chatting to friends and drinking tea.

We stop for a few minutes at a little station set in the middle of a snowy landscape. It is called 'Arctic Circle' because the railway line actually crosses the Arctic Circle at this point. Perhaps this is a good place to get out and stretch our legs? A woman is repairing the line. Many women in Russia are trained as engineers and do many of the skilled and heavy jobs on the railways. As we take a picture of the train it starts to pull away. This is no place to be stranded, and it is quite a chase to get back on the train in time!

As the train moves further north, it is easy to see why local people have started to demonstrate against the pollution from the mining and smelting industries. Huge chimneys pump out great clouds of smoke into the Arctic sky. Acid rain and snow have fallen on the huge lakes and killed many fish.

When we approach Murmansk, it is quite dark, but it is only three o'clock in the afternoon. This far north (Murmansk is the most northerly major city in the world) people live in the 'polar darkness' for some of the winter. For six weeks the sun does not rise above the horizon, and only a weak glow lights up the sky for a short time each day. (Most of the photographs on this page have had to be specially lightened to make them clear).

Today however (7 January), the town does not seem gloomy. In the Russian calendar, today is Christmas Day. The shops are open. Tall dark fir trees sparkle with light in the darkness. We cross the town square, where some children are playing on a castle made of packed snow and ice, to one of the tall block of flats. This is where Sergei and his wife Ludmilla have a small flat. Their son Alexei and his grandmother are in the kitchen making some special cakes called *plushki*. It is Christmas, and party time. Smoked salmon, caviar and champagne are set out on the table. The family watches a service from a Russian Orthodox church on television - it is only recently that Christmas services have been shown on television in Russia.

To complete a Christmas meal, pasties and cranberries will be served in handpainted wooden bowls.

Ships leave Murmansk on the 'polar run', taking fuel, food, furniture and other goods to Arctic islands. In winter the way is cleared by nuclear-powered ice breakers.

The next day we visit the port. There is an important naval base here, as well as shipbuilding and fishing. Sergei's cousin, Mr. Fedosov, captains a nuclear-powered ice breaker that cuts paths through the ice for shipping on the polar routes. Sometimes when the ice breaker, called *Siberia*, stops among the ice floes, polar bears come across the ice to the ship and the crew feed the bears with tins of sweet condensed milk. Sometimes a bear spots an even better meal - a seal - and sets off to stalk its prey. The crew have watched bears cover their black noses with snow to complete their all-white camouflage!

As we leave the port, the snow squeaks under our feet. A giant neon thermometer shows the temperature: $-26^{0}C$. At this temperature, people do not stay out of doors for long, and they certainly need their fur hats to keep them warm. When the temperature drops below $-30^{0}C$, the

MURMANSK

The largest city in the Arctic, located on the northern shore of the Kola peninsula. Approximately 300,000 people live there.

children stay at home and do not go to school.

One evening we meet some school children at a meeting of the Young Pioneers, an organisation rather like Guides and Scouts which many children join. On our last evening we go with them to the Children's Theatre to see a puppet show. The next day, New Year's Day in the Russian calendar, is our last day in Murmansk. Just before we say goodbye, we sit with Sergei and his family for a minute's silence, a way of wishing us a safe journey.

Street scene in Murmansk. The picture of Lenin would probably not be there now, since the break- up of the Soviet Union.

*Reindeer herders
ride through vast
empty landscapes
to keep a check
on their animals.*

YAKUTSK AND BEYOND

Few Westerners have ever been to the remote north-eastern part of Siberia. The city of Yakutsk is the jumping-off point if you want to visit the reindeer herders who live in the coldest part of the Arctic, where winter temperatures may drop to -70°C.

Yakutsk is an old town. It grew up more than 350 years ago, when the Russians travelled east in search of furs. Today, the carved wooden houses, some of them collapsing because of the permafrost, are slowly being replaced with modern blocks. The town sits beside the River Lena, one of three huge rivers that cross Siberia and flow into the Arctic Ocean. A river trip is a good way to pass the time until the flight out to the reindeer herders' camp. A paddle steamer takes visitors to a stone-age site where Sibe-

ria's first inhabitants lived. On the way, the birch forests that border the river are broken up by small farms, where Yakut people raise horses and cattle. In one place the cliffs have been worn away to leave massive stone pillars standing like guards on the river bank.

A little 12-seater plane is the best way to get across the mountains to the small herders' village. The houses, simple wooden cabins, sit beside streets of bare earth. If you look through a window, you will probably find it decorated with moss and dried ferns arranged between the double glazing. Outside, you might find a few tomatoes or cucumbers growing under a polythene cover, and - in a cage - an Arctic fox, being reared for its fur.

Most of the people who live in this remote

*Stone pillars, carved out of the
cliffs by the weather, stand
along the River Lena.*

village are Eveny. They have their own language, but they mostly speak Yakut, and have to learn Russian at school as well. The village has its own school. Some of the children in the school have just come back after spending the long summer holiday with their fathers in the reindeer-herding camps. Family life is not easy for the reindeer herders. For most of the year the children live with their mothers in the village so that they can go to school. The women have jobs in the village - perhaps in the school, in the little hospital or in the fur farm - while their husbands may be 200 miles (320 km) away looking after the reindeer.

The best way to reach one of these camps at this time of year is on horseback. Yakut ponies are very hardy, and good at moving over boggy and stony ground. Much of the land is boggy because the water from the melting snow cannot drain through the permafrost. At the camp, six canvas tents - these used to be made of reindeer hide - are pitched on flat grassy ground beside a river. One man is throwing stones into the water to catch fish for supper. An elderly woman, one of the 'tentkeepers' who look after the camp, has collected fungi and wild berries, and reindeer milk for tea.

Reindeer milk is whisked with a piece of antler pierced with holes to make a frothy drink.

Today the children of reindeer herders stay in the village to attend school. In the past, the whole family moved from one camp to the next with their reindeer.

Reindeer herders feed the animals with salt.

Everyone sleeps on reindeer hides which are laid over the larch branches covering the floor of the tent. The tents are quite bare. The herders have few possessions with them, because they have to move camp several times a year. So little grows here that to find enough to eat each reindeer needs 150 acres (52 hectares) - 0.2 square miles (0.6 sq km) or 300 football pitches - of pasture. Each camp has about 2,000 reindeer, spread out vast areas of empty landscape.

Early the next morning the herders set off - some on horseback and others riding reindeer - to round up more of the herd. They recognise their own animals by special marks or coloured ribbons in their ears. They check the reindeer to make sure they are healthy, vaccinate them against disease, saw off the antlers of the male reindeer and decide which ones to send for slaughter. The antlers are now sold to Japan to make medicine.

Later, when the roundup is finished, the reindeer will be released again. When the winter sets in, the herders will track their animals by snowmobile. Then the horses are set free to live in the wild for seven months of the year. The herders leave their animals to fend for themselves in winter because the short summers do not allow them to grow any crops so they are not able to provide food for them.

As the reindeer herders prepare to move camp, we prepare to leave the Siberian Arctic. We have completed our journey round the Arctic Circle. Kotzebue, our starting point, lies just a few hundred miles to the east, across the Bering Strait. We have travelled across all kinds of landscapes, from the golden larch forests of Siberia to the treeless tundra of Alaska. We have met all kinds of Arctic people, from the Dene to the Saami. We have heard different languages and eaten different foods, lived in different kinds of homes and worn all kinds of clothes. Yet, all through this 50,000 mile (80,000 km) journey, the people who live round the Arctic Circle have shown they have much in common. Perhaps the thing we will remember most clearly is the way they live in harmony with their environment, working with each other and with nature in their struggle to survive Arctic conditions and the added stresses brought upon them by pollution.

Animals of the Arctic

The brown or grizzly bear, found in Siberia, Alaska and Western Canada makes a den in winter and sleeps until spring, surviving from its body fat reserves. It has a diet of salmon, rodents, roots and berries.

The silver fox is hunted for its snow-white coat in winter. In the summer it moves to the area where melting tundra meets the tree line, and its coat changes to a grey-brown colour to match its new environment.

Snowy owls live in the open and feed on lemmings, crustaceans, and fish. They are strong enough to catch Arctic hare. Their habitat is North America, Asia and northern Europe.

The polar bear is an endangered species so there are strict quotas for hunting. This privilege is usually given to the Inuit. Polar bears are found in northern Alaska, Canada, Greenland and the Russian Arctic.

A sea otter relaxing after being cleaned following the Exxon Valdez oil tanker spillage off the coast of Alaska. These marine mammals are fascinating to watch while resting, playing or feeding in the sea. They were once almost hunted to extinction.

The narwhal, known as the Sea Unicorn, has a long ivory tusk, whose use is still a mystery. It is found only in the high Arctic areas of Canada and feeds at the edge of the pack-ice on halibut and polar cod.

INDEX

Numbers in bold show pages with pictures.

GLOSSARY OF ARCTIC TERMS

(Not all these terms are used in this book, but you may find them in
other writing about the Arctic)

Acid rain/snow — rain or snow containing a sulphur and nitrogen mixture, which kills plants and fishes; caused by burning coal and oil.

Arctic circle — a parallel of latitude at 60 degrees 33 minutes north, marking the limit of the North Frigid Zone.

Arctic haze — a layer of soot blown by the wind from industrialised countries which accumulates in the Arctic atmosphere and changes the colours of sunsets.

Aurora Borealis — northern lights produced by charged electrons and protons striking gas particles in the Earth's upper atmosphere.

Blubber — layer of fat under the skin of some sea animals e.g. seals. It helps the animal keep warm and is used by the Inuit for fuel and fat.

Boreal — forest areas and tundras of the north and Arctic region.

Bush doctor — doctor who flies in light aircraft to isolated villages.

Cache — food storage unit, made of wooden logs on stilts usually reached by a ladder, to protect food from marauding animals.

Caribou — American reindeer.

Chill factor — wind can lower the effective temperature by many degrees.

Dene — native word for indian tribes, i.e. Dogrib, Cree, Chippewyan, Slave, Yellowknife, Hare, etc.

Frostbite — damage to the body by extremely cold temperatures.

Geothermal (energy) — heating and lighting produced by hot water from volcanic activity.

Glaciers — slow-moving rivers of ice, formed over many years when more snow falls than melts.

Global warming — the heating up of our planet due to industrial and fossil fuel pollutants in the atmosphere; could melt the ice-caps and raise sea levels.

Greenlandic — the language of Greenland, a dialect of the Inuit language.

Greenlanders — the people of Greenland: descended from the Inuit of North America and Europeans from Denmark and Norway.

Icebreaker — large strong ship for clearing channels in the ice pack for ships voyaging the Arctic Ocean.

Ice floe — a sheet of floating sea ice.

Igloo — Inuit word for house or home (snowhouse).

Iglu — stone and turf house.

Indigenous — occurring or living naturally in an area; not introduced from outside; 'native'.

Inuk — an "eskimo". The word means "human being", a "real man". *Plural:* **Inuit**.

Inuktitut — the way an Inuk does things. You can add 'titut' to any word. If you wanted to say 'the way an Englishman does things' it would be 'Englishtitut'.

Inuktitut — language spoken by Inuit (Can.).

Joiking — Saami style of singing.

Kamiks — boots made out of skin (Canadian Inuit).

Kayak — traditional Inuit boat made from stretched seal skin over wooden or bone framework, used for hunting at sea.

Komatik — (Inuit) sledge.

Lasso — a long rope with a noose on the end used for catching animals.

Lava — molten rock, from volcanoes or fissures in the earth's crust.

Lichen — fungus/algae plant, food for animals on the tundra.

Mukluks — lightweight boots made from seal, caribou or moosehide, warm in extreme cold.

Muktuk — the skin of whale, walrus or narwhal, rich in protein and vitamins; tastes like coconut.

Muskrat — large member of the rat family which lives in water, common throughout North America and named after its 'musky' smell.

Ozone layer — blanket of protective gases which surrounds the earth and prevents harmful rays from the sun damaging living things.

Parka — traditional Inuit garment made of skin, also modern ones of synthetic material.

Permafrost — frozen ground, which remains frozen for two years or more.

Polar night — a period of several weeks every year in winter when the sun does not rise above the horizon north of the Arctic Circle.

Potlatch — Indian custom, a celebration with singing, dancing, exchanges and feasting.

Saami — the people of Saamiland, formerly called 'Lapps'.

Satellite dish — metal dish on ground to communicate with space satellites for weather and aircraft communications.

Sedna — Inuit goddess of the sea.

Shaman — spiritual leader, wise man.

Sila — a spiritual presence, the most influential God in the Inuit world.

Skidoo — a kind of motorised sledge with runners and caterpillar tracks instead of wheels.

Sledge — for carrying people or goods across snow and ice, pulled by dogs, reindeer or snowmobile.

Snowmobile — a petrol-driven vehicle designed for use on ice and snow, one make of which is the Skidoo.

Spinner — a bright piece of metal or wood tied to a fishing line and used to attract fish.

Teepee — a kind of tent made of canvas or animal skins stretched over poles.

Throat singing — Inuit singing (about everday life and legends), using only the sounds coming from the throat.

Treeline — the line around the earth, north of which there is not enough light for trees to grow; or the level on a mountain above which trees cannot grow.

Tundra — vast flat almost treeless plains with low-growing arctic vegetation.

Tupilak — Inuit Spirit, ghost.

Ulo/Ulu — a traditional Inuit woman's knife of wood, bone and steel. For cutting up and skinning animals.

Umiak — Inuit walrus skin boats which carry 10-12 people, powered by paddles or outboard motors.

Wind chill factor — wind can lower the effective temperature by many degrees, causing possible frostbite.